I dedicate this book to my three children: Yaahl Xanjuuwaas, Huuts Swansang, and
Kwiigeeiiwans. Dalang dii ḵuyaadaa g̱usdlang, I love you all very much.
Haw'aa for listening to me tell this story the whole time you were growing up.
Haw'aa for choosing me to be dalang Aaw, your mom.

Editors: Emma Bullen and Echo Armstrong
Text & illustration copyright © Medicine Wheel Education Inc. 2016
ISBN-978-0-9938694-6-4
For more information about this book and others, visit us at www.medicinewheel.education

Yaahl (the Raven) created the Earth and made it beautiful with all the waters of the oceans and rivers. He made trees, orcas, bears and even all the two-leggeds to share in its beauty. He brought the great light to shine upon the Earth. Then he rested.

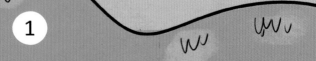

Yaahl spent his time in a quiet place on Haida Gwaii where he watched
all the beings live and grow. But a feeling was also growing inside him— a feeling
he didn't quite understand. Yaahl felt the need to start building,
and soon he was building big cedar Xaads Nee (Haida houses). He loved building these
great houses so much that he barely noticed that 50 years had passed.

4

Yaahl wondered, "Why am I building so many houses when I am the only one living here?" He thought the answer might have something to do with the feeling that had been growing inside him. Yaahl trusted this feeling, so he knew that it was time to stop building.

6

Yaahl had been so distracted by the feeling, he didn't realize it was almost winter!
Hurriedly, he gathered and dried food.
He also gathered ts'uu gid (red cedar). When winter arrived,
he began making the cedar into a sleeping mat and
a cape to cover his shoulders.

When Yaahl finished his work, he sat and pondered the feeling inside him, and his understanding of it grew.

He wondered about all the two-leggeds, and he realized, "I'm feeling lonely, quite lonely, for the company of other people."

Yaahl knew what he had to do to ease his loneliness. "I'll have a feast," he thought, "and I'll invite all the two-leggeds from all four of the directions to join me." Although Yaahl had enough houses to host all the people, he knew he did not have enough food to offer his guests.

Yaahl hunted and fished, then he carefully smoked and dried the meat. He wanted only the best for his guests. He gathered clams and berries in the kaadii (baskets) he had made during the long winter nights. He stored the food with great care so that nothing would spoil.

Yaahl was just about to invite his guests to the feast when he realized he did not have any gifts to offer people.

Once again, Yaahl took up his bone tools and harvested cedar. He brought back the materials he gathered and got to work. He made only the best baskets, hats, mats, capes, and skirts to honour the people from all four directions — East, South, West and North.

When he was done building the great houses and preparing the food and gifts, he knew it was time to call the people.

Yaahl faced towards the East. He stomped his foot four times and called out,
"Swansang (one), sdang (two), hlunahl (three), stangsang (four)!" He looked to the horizon,
and he saw canoes filled with all the Native people rowing towards the shores of Haida Gwaii.
Each of them wore items that represented their distinct nation, and each of them spoke
their distinct language. Each group had its own unique culture.
Each culture was special in its own way.

Yaahl faced towards the South. He stomped his foot four times and called out,
"Swansang (one), sdang (two), hlunahl (three), stangsang (four)!" He looked to the horizon,
and he saw canoes filled with all the Asian people rowing towards the shores of Haida Gwaii.
Each of them wore items that represented their distinct nation, and each of them spoke
their distinct language. Each group had its own unique culture.
Each culture was special in its own way.

Yaahl faced towards the West. He stomped his foot four times and called out, "Swansang (one), sdang (two), hlunahl (three), stangsang (four)!" He looked to the horizon, and he saw canoes filled with all the African people rowing towards the shores of Haida Gwaii. Each of them wore items that represented their distinct nation, and each of them spoke their distinct language. Each group had its own unique culture. Each culture was special in its own way."

Yaahl faced towards the North. He stomped his foot four times and called out, "Swansang (one), sdang (two), hlunahl (three), stangsang (four)!" He looked to the horizon, and he saw canoes filled with all the European people rowing towards the shores of Haida Gwaii. Each of them wore items that represented their distinct nation, and each of them spoke their distinct language. Each group had its own unique culture. Each culture was special in its own way.

Yaahl welcomed everyone to the feast by saying "Dalang ky'uusii aats'uugaa" (Each and every one of you is welcome here). He introduced all the nations from each of the four directions — East, South, West, and North — to each other. All nations saw they had different and unique cultures and that each culture was special.

The people started dancing, singing and making the music that was unique to their nation's culture. They also started to learn about other nation's cultures. All the people loved the gifts Yaahl had made for them. They feasted and feasted. Days turned into weeks, weeks turned into months, and months turned into years.

At the end of the feast, before each nation returned to its land, the people were given a great gift even greater than the gifts of baskets, mats, and hats. Yaahl gave each person a unique and special gift that they could carry in their hearts. Yaahl knew that each person would share this gift with all the world.

When we were born, all of us were invited to Yaahl's feast, and all of us were given a special gift to share with the world. Some of us are good at hunting or carving, others are good at fishing or dancing or anything else you might imagine.

It is up to each one of us to find the gift Yaahl has placed in our hearts and to help others find their gifts. When we do this, we show people how to listen to themselves, the spirits, and the Salaana (Creator).

When you learn to love yourself completely inside and out, you will be able to share with the world the gift Yaahl gave you. People will look to you to help them find their gift from Yaahl. You will learn to say, "Dii dii ḵuyaadang" (I love me) to yourself and "Dang dii ḵuyaadang" (I love you) to others.

We are perfectly imperfect beings who continue to grow with our gifts from Yaahl.

## Haida Words & Their Meanings

Yaahl (yaw-hl) – Raven

Xaads nee (haw-ds nay) – Haida house

Ts'uu gid (ch-u-gid) – Red cedar

Kaadii (kaw-dee) – Baskets

Salaana ( suh-laa-n) – Creator

Swansang (swan-sung) - One

Sdang (sduh-ung) - Two

Hlunahl (hl-uh-nahl) - Three

Stansang (stan-sung) - Four

Haw'aa (how-uh) - Thank you

## Conversation Starters

What did the Raven do in the story?

Do you remember the Raven's name?

Why did the Raven throw a feast?

What did the Raven need to throw a feast?

If you were throwing a big feast, who would you invite?

Can you think of a song you'd sing at the feast?

Do you know what your special gift is?

How do you think you might find out what your special gift is?

## About the Author

Kung Jaadee (Roberta Kennedy) is a traditional Haida storyteller, singer and drummer from Haida Gwaii in Northern British Columbia. She teaches Xaad Kil/Haida language and culture five days a week. For more than 24 years, she has delighted audiences across Canada at festivals, schools, museums, aboriginal celebrations, and conferences. Kung Jaadee loves singing her traditional Haida songs, drumming, laughing, baking, and learning more about her language. Her name was presented to her at her great uncle's memorial feast by her cousin, Crystal Robinson, and means 'Moon Woman'.

A book from Medicine Wheel Education

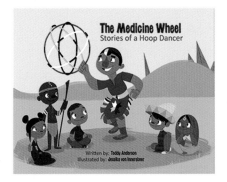

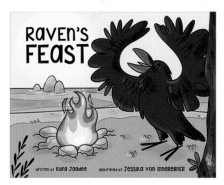

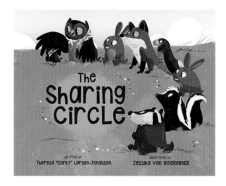

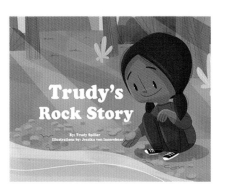

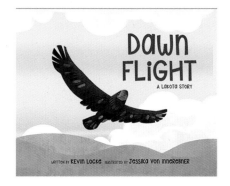

Books for ages 7-12 (available in English and French)

Educational lesson plans and posters
available online!